GOD's INVITATION

- ♦ Your child is like you. Your child is different from you. This is why your child is so precious and so difficult. At times you would die for your child and at other times you think your child will be the death of you.

- ♦ YOUR CHILD ~ GOD'S INVITATION offers fresh insight into the unique relationship – always loving but often painful – between you and your child. The bond you share is a link into the bond between God and yourself. In fact, the two relationships are very much alike.

- ♦ YOUR CHILD ~ GOD'S INVITATION offers a window into a spirituality which has its origin in your own experiences as a parent and you may be surprised to find yourself looking at those experiences in a very different way.

- ♦ YOUR CHILD ~ GOD'S INVITATION also offers help to parents who are preparing their children for celebrations such as Baptism, First Holy Communion and Confirmation.

YOUR CHILD

Your child – God's invitation – began with the conception and birth of your baby. The relationship formed between you and your child means that life is changed for ever.

AN INVITATION TO GROW

66 *A woman in childbirth suffers, because her time has come; but when she has given birth to the child she forgets the suffering in her joy that a person has been born into the world. So it is with you: you are sad now, but I shall see you again, and your hearts will be full of joy, and that joy no one shall take* 99 *from you.*

HAVING MY FIRST CHILD . . .

◆ *"Was a shock! At the time we weren't planning a baby. We were in a one-bedroomed flat and had planned to move to something bigger before starting a family. After the shock I felt, 'Yes, great!'"*

◆ *"I wanted a boy to play sport with. But then Jenny was in hospital a lot before the baby arrived. I was scared. I had never before experienced someone so close to me so ill and that upset me terribly."*

◆ *"I was elated and fearful because of the responsibility for a new life. I worried about what would go wrong."*

◆ *"I was thrilled and excited."*

◆ *"I wasn't married at the time so the pregnancy was a shock. It was made clear to me I didn't need to keep the baby. It wasn't the baby's fault I was pregnant and once I'd made the decision to keep her I was much happier."*

◆ *"Soon after Michael was born I was handed this crib which had a note on it, 'Next feed due 7.30am'. It was 7.25 and I thought, 'It's down to me. This tiny bundle is down to me'. It was great."*

◆ *"We waited a long time – eight years. This made our first child momentous. At first, I felt elation: then, 'what have we done?' That was when we realised there was no turning back. I was afraid I wouldn't be up to it. It was for the rest of my life. It was leaping into the unknown."*

Having a child can be exciting but it is also scary. This tiny creature seems to take over your whole life – and it's exhausting. You discover that being a parent is the one job you can't resign from and responsibility takes on a whole new meaning. That's why there are times when parents find it very hard and can even resent their job. But there's another side to the picture. A child can take so much out of you yet can also draw out of you so many unsuspected talents.

NO FEAR!

Many of the games we play with our baby create great laughter and many chuckles. In every case – tickling, throwing the baby up in the air, bouncing on your knees or saying 'boo' – the action is potentially frightening. But your baby feels safe with you, trusts you, relies completely on your care. The result is that the "fear" is redeemed by loving confidence and laughter is the result. Trusting love casts out fear.

"What are you going to call it?"

When you announced you were expecting a baby there was probably at least one person who asked you, "What are you going to call it?" as though your baby was a thing rather than a person. The greatest insult is to call someone "it". A baby is not "it". A baby is "someone". And that makes all the difference in the world. We can take or leave "it". It is only with "someone" that we can be drawn into a relationship that changes us.

Recognition at last

It's great when your child recognises you, lets people know who you are. Didn't you secretly long for the day when you first heard, "Mama" or "Dada"? It probably seemed ages before you heard it. All babies start by babbling and it's only gradually that they successfully form such a difficult word as "Dada". But it takes much, much longer for your child to identify the word "Dada" with the real thing. Mama, Mummy, Mam, Dada, Dad, Daddy – all mean so much more than the word alone. As the years pass they conjure up all that is at the heart of our beginnings, all that tells us who we are, where we belong.

For followers of Jesus Christ, God is not an "It". God is "Someone". And God is Someone who invites us into a relationship similar to the relationship our children have with us. It is Jesus Christ who reveals this. Just as God is the Father of Jesus so God is also our parent.

The precious closeness between baby and parent is the relationship that God seeks with each one of us. Long-winded prayers — "babbling" as Jesus called it — have as little effect with God as they do with us. Our first words are "Mama" or "Dada". These are the first words that God our Father also longs to hear from us. There is only one thing God longs for; words revealing a recognition of our relationship with him as our loving parent — just as those key words confirmed our baby's real relationship with us.

YOUR CHILD AT THE HEART OF CREATION

As a parent you discover and rediscover personal gifts in yourself — gifts that you never realised you had. You are probably surprised at what you managed to cope with and the way your child has grown and developed. In fact, you are experiencing the delicate unfolding of your own potential as a child of God. When you were younger you were probably aware of the world around you – its beauty, its life, its dangers. But with the birth of your child you are beginning to enter into the heart of creation; you are part of creation in a new yet very real and active sense. You have the gift of a child from God. Everything has come together in and through your body and a child has been born – a child who has been entrusted to you by God. God believes in you. God knows you have the potential, the gifts, to nurture and love his new creation into full life.

You have so much to offer

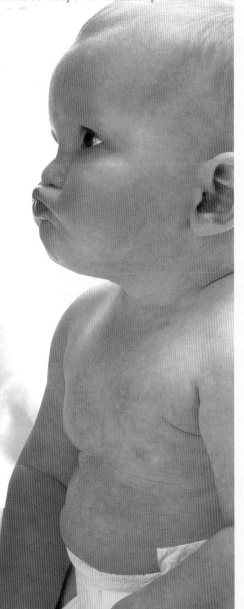

♦ "I have discovered I have patience. I never knew I had so much."

♦ "My child thinks the world of me. I didn't know I was capable of giving and receiving so much love."

♦ "Having your children looking up to you and admiring you and wanting to be with you – is wonderful."

♦ "I wouldn't have thought I could possibly be so devoted to so many people – I can talk to each child but each one differently."

♦ "Having children has given me more insight into other peoples' difficulties."

♦ "I was afraid I wouldn't be up to it – but so far I am coping."

♦ "Being responsible for this little helpless person has revealed to me a tolerance and willingness to adapt that I didn't think I had."

♦ "I can get up at the most unearthly hours after all!"

3

Yⁿᵘᴿ CHILD

Your child –
God's invitation –
is the fruit of
partnership.
Usually – though
not always – this
partnership of
man and woman is
a loving one.
But, whatever the
quality of love,
your child can
lead to a deeper
appreciation
of the partnership
between God and
ourselves.

AN INVITATION TO GROW

> *66 You did not choose
> me,
> no, I chose you;
> and I commissioned
> you to go out and to
> bear fruit,
> fruit that will last. 99*

Words of Jesus Christ to his
followers

HOW DO YOU CHOOSE A PERMANENT PARTNER?

Sexual attraction is obviously important. So are personal qualities though here the coming together is often like that of magnets – the attraction of opposites. An extrovert, perhaps, will go for a partner who is more introvert; someone keen on spor may be drawn to someone whose limit of physical activity is opening a can of lager.

If it's only sexual attraction which brings two people together the partnership won't last. Nor will it survive a child. Having a child can be a good time to take a fresh loo at the partnership and how each other feels about it. For a child means that a couple forced to spend less time face to face as lovers and spend more time side by side as friends looking beyond themselves to their child and the outside world. Many – perhaps most – couples discover that children test their love.

*"**Children** drove a coach and horses through my relationship with Michael. It was a while before we had children and when we did they became the core of discussion together. Now I wonder, and worry, whether we'll function as a couple when the children move on."*

*"**Children have meant** that I've less time to myself – also the fact that I'm always tired and broke. On the other hand this means that the time Gill and myself do spend together is more precious."*

*"**Keith and I** were friends before we thought about marriage (though we disliked each other at first) so children haven't upset that."*

*"**Gerry has tired** of bringing up a family before I have so I feel alone in bringing up the younger children. But to be honest I think the way I do things is best – so in a sense I'm only doing what I want and having to accept the consequences."*

*"**It was five years** before we start a family. It did us good to have time together – it was a good rock before starting a family. There was a lot of wate under the bridge before the rocky time started."*

AS PARTI

Did you choose or were you chosen?

Your child didn't choose to be born. Many children, in moments of anger, shout this fact to their parents. Parents, in responding to such anger, may be tempted to shout back: "Neither did I choose you!" But nothing can be more disastrous for the child seeking security. The fact is that any child who is to grow, even if they didn't choose to be born, must feel chosen. (Any child who is adopted, of course, has a unique experience of what it means to be chosen in a particularly special way.)

This feeling of being "chosen" is equally important for every couple. So often both partners flounder on the conviction that they made a bad choice or a good choice of partner – and both are equally disastrous. For there is a world of difference between choosing and being chosen. "Choosing" leads to choosiness, to self-satisfaction and the worst form of taking – taking for granted. Being "chosen" leads to appreciation.

How do you choose a permanent partner? The fact is you can't. Children can help parents to change their appreciation of each other from "This is the one I chose" to "I have been chosen by this person". This realisation changes a temporary relationship conditional on what "I choose" to a relationship which is permanent and unconditional.

The existence of your child is a confirmation of the mystical and eternal elements at work in your relationship. Often such elements are overlooked and the sexuality expressed has an incompleteness which can be painful or confusing.

Yet sex between two people which is a true reflection of genuine love is the nearest experience we can have on this earth of heaven. It is God's gift to us. The creation of a child is the completion of the experience —we have become partners with the Creator in creation.

"Annie thinks the world of me – I didn't know I was capable of giving and receiving so much love."

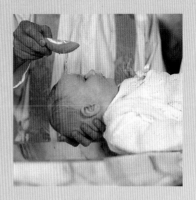

YOUR CHILD AND BAPTISM

The water poured out at Baptism is a sign of God's life-giving love. Baptism, a ceremony common to all Christians, is basically a "mutual admiration" ceremony. The heavenly Father shares our admiration of our child. During Baptism there are a number of other occasions when this love is recalled. For followers of Jesus Christ, then, Baptism is a ceremony which makes real what we might easily forget; the life and love between God and ourselves, like the life and love between you and your child, is for ever, whatever the cost.

Annie thinks her daddy is great. And, it has to be said, David thinks Annie is wonderful. Most nights before he goes to bed he goes into her room for a few minutes and watches her quietly sleeping. The mutual admiration (Penny, David's wife, calls it "adoration") is mostly unspoken because Annie is still only two. But she already has a will of her own and every morning Annie scrambles into her parents' bed while David and Penny try not to notice and sleep on.

Some people believe that God only loves us when we are good, in other words, that he is nowhere near as good at loving as we are. Jesus Christ made it clear that this was a daft belief. He then went to great lengths to reassure us over and over again that God loves us more than any human parent. In the end the cost of such love was his own death, freely accepted in order to prove his point.

This doesn't mean that God only loves those who are baptised. It's just that he doesn't want the secret love that he has for every human being to remain a secret. It doesn't mean a great deal to Annie that her father watches her sleeping in bed every night. For her, the morning is much more fun when she can enjoy the feel of cuddling up into her father's arms. Baptism is just one precious moment when God 'touches' his child. One such moment in a lifetime, of course, is hardly enough.

Your child will have forced you to see your relationship with your partner in a new way. In some areas it may have deepened your relationship and, in other respects, it will have caused difficulties. A partnership is never easy. It is often said that children keep a couple together. This may be true but children can't be used simply as cement. If a couple stay together solely for the sake of the children tension can lead to the whole structure crumbling and everyone is hurt.

YOUR CHILD

Your child –
God's invitation –
takes us to a
place we would
never otherwise
discover. This is
the fruit of living
in intimacy with
others.

AN INVITATION TO
GROW

" *Father, may they be
one in us, as you are
in me and I am in
you, so that the
world may believe it
was you who sent
me... may they be so
completely one that
the world will realise
that it was you who
sent me and that I
have loved them as
much as you loved
me.* "

Part of the prayer of Jesus
Christ for his friends on the
night before he died

AS A FAM

EVERY FAMILY IS DIFFERENT

But in all families one thing remains the same: your child means that you live with the unexpected.

As a parent you will remember the moments when your small child said the unexpected thing everybody laughed; and the moments, too, when your much older child said the unexpected thing and everyone glowered. That's family life – young children can get away w almost anything.

The unexpected brings pains and pleasures – usually lots of both. And this brings most pare to a most unexpected discovery. The pain is usually worth the pleasure. Sometimes, parents say that life would be happier without children – but this is quite rare. As a parent you give up much yet you wouldn't have it any different.

Vivien – separated with five children
"When I got married I pictured a nice happy family home, everyone playing together, having conversations at the lunch-table, doing everything together. It's not like that at all! But I would swop the children for anything. Recently, someone asked my why? Why does anyone love children? Because they're mine – they're part of me."

Catherine – married with three children
"When Ruth was an adolescent I used to get angry with her – she was very moody. But I cou remember what I was like and found myself saying the same things that my mother had said me. Now I have a very close relationship with her – we get angry about the same things."

David – married with two children
"When I was younger I resented the responsibility of children and the fact that we couldn't aff so much because of them. Now I give more and expect less – that makes it easier. I realise ne that they're not going to turn out as I want but I think I've learned to accept that."

inding happiness

e "perfect family" only exists in the fantasy world. The reality of every family is constant
sis and tension. This is because every family reflects the family of the human race.
ess you lock yourselves away in a nuclear cellar your family is touched by the outside world.
e door of your home is the interface between the community you are trying to create and the
nmunity of the human family. You can't turn your home into a castle where your family remains
ouched by what's happening elsewhere.

ir struggle for a happier family, then, is much wider than your own home. You can only sit back
isfied that yours is the ideal family when every other family in the world can do the same. There
i Jewish proverb: "There are rich and poor in the world so that the rich can help the poor."
e giving demanded by family life can be painful; but it is only through such help that we find
piness.

YOUR CHILD AND FIRST HOLY COMMUNION

First Holy Communion Day is a day when children experience saying "thank you" to God. This "thank you" is not a polite note for some new toy but a "thank you" for the gift of love and everything in life.

When children start receiving Communion they're old enough to realise that life includes many difficulties. Many of these difficulties come from their being caught up in the life of others. They are beginning to realise that they are not the centre of the universe; they can't live their lives doing just what they want.

Holy Communion is a time when followers of Jesus learn that their lives are caught up also in the life of God; and God's life is caught up in their's. They are learning that Jesus, the Lord, is still living as a human being. In Communion he is present in a special yet intimate way to each of his brothers and sisters – the children of God.

Many people question how Jesus can be present in the signs of bread and wine. This is an important question which takes us to the heart of our faith that God is truly present in our world. What is more important is why Jesus continues to make himself present. His answer is the same as why Vivien gives herself to her children – "because they're mine...they're part of me".

Finding happiness ~ God's way

There is no difference between our way and God's way of finding happiness. The way is through giving. The advice of Jesus Christ on how to find happiness comes, significantly, at the very beginning of his teaching. It's in the family that giving is often most painful but also brings most happiness.

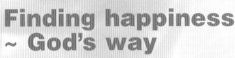

GROWING AS A FAMILY MEANS...

recognising that love is priceless
"How happy are the poor in spirit; theirs is the kingdom of heaven."
Jesus Christ

sharing kindness
"Happy the gentle; they shall have the earth for their heritage."
Jesus Christ

crying – and laughing – together
"Happy those who mourn; they shall be comforted."
Jesus Christ

working for what really matters
"Happy those who hunger and thirst for what is right; they shall be satisfied."
Jesus Christ

accepting differences
"Happy the merciful; they shall have mercy shown them."
Jesus Christ

seeking honesty
"Happy the pure in heart; they shall see God."
Jesus Christ

discovering truth
"Happy the peacemakers; they shall be called children of God."
Jesus Christ

seeing beyond the present
"Happy those who are persecuted in the cause of right; theirs is the kingdom of heaven."
Jesus Christ

*ant my children to grow up to appreciate the good things in life. I don't want them
er-wealthy but to be grateful for what they have. When I left food at home my mother
d to shout at me that lots of children are starving and I replied that I'll put the food in
envelope and send it to them. That was flippant but it's important they appreciate what
y've got. I want my children to be more appreciative than I am."*

e most parents Derek doesn't want his children to be super-wealthy. He wants
m to be happy. Appreciative people are usually happy people. That is why
ents spend so much time teaching their children to say, "thank you".

Your child – God's invitation – may seem to break you and make you as you search for ways to stay together.

AN INVITATION TO GROW IN FOR

> 66 *It was only right we should celebrate and rejoice, because your brother here was dead and has come to life; he was lost and is found.* 99
>
> Jesus Christ

"They had been to 'everybody else's party' and they must now have one of their own. they decided to have a joint one with some friends in order to make it a really big affair. No need for us to worry, they would prepare and organise it for themselves...

Why didn't I go and stay with my sister for the weekend? I drew the line at leaving the entire house and contents to their mercy but agreed to keep out of the way in my bedroom.

The bathroom is next to my bedroom and, as the evening wore on, a queue formed on the landing. Blissfully unaware of the 'old lady' in the bedroom they chatted freely. My hair needed no curling tongs that night! It curled twice over. Were my children really friends with these people? Did they really do that? Are they in agreement with the views expressed? My heart sank as I heard my own childrens' voices. Their good home and Christian upbringing seemed completely wasted. It was agony lying there, not being able to do or say anything."

These parents experience the agony every loving parent has to suffer.

Having taught their children Christian values, given them love and good example, they had to stand back and allow them to be ignored if their children chose; they had to let them make their own mistakes.

How painful it can be, but what a lesson we can learn from it, for aren't we all "spiritual teenagers"? Our heavenly parent, God, loves us and gives us many gifts and opportunities. He gives us life and all that we need to make the most of it. Then he stands back to enable us to grow to maturity, to be free to choose which way we want to go. Like the parent at the party, he is present yet unseen. He sees the wrong and foolish things we do; he hears us reject so much of what he has taught us; yet he understands that we often learn only through our mistakes and sufferings. And so he keeps out of the way. But he doesn't turn away from us; he is listening and suffers the pain and anxiety of all parents as he watches his children grow.

VENESS

"Brr...Brrr...Brr...

the phone rang insistently.
'Hello, Teresa? No, I don't think so, hang on a minute, I'll ask her.'
'Who on earth is it at this time?'
'It's Teresa's parents, she hasn't been home since this morning, they are wondering if our Sue has seen or heard from her.'

I looked at my watch, it was after midnight as I shook a sleepy Sue. No, she hadn't seen anything of Teresa for a couple of days. The next evening I asked Sue if there was any further news of Teresa.

'Oh yes, she turned up at her boyfriend's place.'
'Didn't she know how worried her parents were?'
'I suppose so, she was fed up with them getting on at her.'

I thought how painful parenthood is. Teresa, so wrapped up in herself, completely failed to grasp the depth of her parents' love and concern. She saw it only as a restriction, a hindrance and a limitation to her freedom. I suppose such attitudes are a familiar part of living with adolescents, they are part of growing up."

Next time we feel our children have driven us to breaking point, it may help to remember God's infinite patience with ourselves.

Faith is our recognition of our dependence on God. His love for us is there but we don't recognise it. As a parent you are trying to share your love and the results of your experience with your child but it's impossible for your teenager to fully understand because of their immaturity and their limited growth. In fact, you are experiencing something of God's frustration as a Parent!

The truth is that, before God, most of us are adolescents. This is nothing to be ashamed of. Adolescence is a stage of growth we all have to go through. But if we recognise that our frustration as parents is mirrored by the anxiety of God about his Prodigal son, we have reached a milestone in our growth. We can begin to look differently at things.

Your Child and Reconciliation

"Christopher has taken to spending periods away from home with his mates and there's times when I want him to get out of my life altogether. But when he's not around I wonder what he's up to. I'm constantly thinking this – so I realise I haven't totally disregarded him. I still love him."

Learning to live together takes a lifetime. This is because forgiving is the hardest form of giving; and our desire for independence makes us reluctant to ask for more than we have to – so saying "sorry" is the hardest word.

The Sacrament of Reconciliation (many people still call it "Confession") is the way in which Christians try to develop their own understanding and practice of forgiveness. This is done by recognising and experiencing God's continual loving patience and forgiveness of ourselves.

Such forgiveness is a permanent fact of his relationship with us and it is one which you will readily understand as a parent – even when your child lets you down, betrays you or hurts you, you still love that child, even in your pain.

So it is with God.

Saying "sorry" is part of family life and part of the life of God's family. It's a word we try to avoid because it means admitting we were wrong – sometimes very wrong. But it's also a word that leads us to dig deeper into a relationship. It can lead us to sit down and talk through what's gone wrong so that, through the hurt and even betrayal, there is a new understanding. Through the wound the relationship is not only healed or restored but is strengthened. In the celebration of confession your child is encouraged to sit down with God and, in saying sorry, to enjoy the feeling and fact of true reconciliation.

YOUR CHILD

AN INVITATION TO GROW

**Your child –
God's invitation –
lifts you
into a
wider world.**

IN

THE KEY TO UNDERSTANDING

We cannot begin to understand anyone else until we learn to understand ourselves. And that is one of the great advantages parents of teenagers have; in the middle of life you are often thrown into confusion and self-doubt which forces you to begin to question your own attitudes, values and faith.

You have reached a crossroad in your life. And this can be the beginning of a whole new range of opportunities and growth if you can begin to trust God and believe that he cares about you just as much and more than you care about your teenager.

*66 Go out to the whole
world;
proclaim the good
news to all
creation...
Teach them to
observe all the
commands I gave
you.
And know that I am
with you always;
yes, to the end of
time. 99*

The final word of Jesus.

● *"When my husband walked out on us I felt that the bottom had dropped out of the world. My three teenagers were already more than a handful, the eldest was messing about at college and not really getting to grips with any work. The second was besotted by a girl at school and forever coming in late. The third was just rude, unhelpful and bone idle. My husband going was the last straw. We had always been a happy family. We had our ups and downs, yes, but I had done my best to be a good parent although it had been hard at times. Your children never seem to notice the trouble you go to in order to give them a good start.*

I fell apart. Suddenly, I no longer cared whether they came or went, washed or stayed dirty, worked or just messed about, went to church on Sunday or gave up the faith. I gave up the struggle to do the right thing, be a good parent or even a good Christian...

My teenagers saved my life. They didn't change overnight into angels, but they supported me, made an effort with the washing, cooking and general running of the home. They didn't seem to mind if I was a failure – they just loved me and tried to show me that in their often awkward, self-conscious way. They made Christ real to me. Once I gave up trying to be a perfect parent it gave them a chance to come close to me in my vulnerability and weakness."

Most parents escape the collapse that this last mother suffered, yet the vast majority of parents do go through a similar experience of 'wanting to give up'. This can be important as we grow in the Christian life.

What does this mean in practice? The fact is that being a parent is seen as an adult, mature role. It means that you spend a significant number of years being 'in charge' – from deciding which nappies or baby foods to use, which schools and the kind of family life you want. This brings with it an occupational hazard: we can begin to believe that we are in charge of everything, especially if we have taken being a parent seriously. It comes as a shock, then, to discover that as our family grows our control seems to be slipping. Meanwhile, during those years of 'control' we have probably lost sight of the child within ourselves who may still need to do some growing up, may still need some maturing and will certainly need some encouragement to keep going.

VE

Like children leaving home in any family God allows us to make a life and a world for ourselves though we continue in the support of his love.

- *"There's times when I'm tempted to whack Ian round the head – though I'd have to stand on a chair to do it.*
He's exactly how we've made him – he's independent. We've always tried to give him responsibility though there's times when he's selfish and thinks the world revolves around him. He never talks when the other children are around – he likes to have me to himself."

Children bring tension. Dependence begins to break into independence. This means lots of sullen silence, broken by wars of words. Because tension is always unpleasant most people look for someone to blame. Teenagers and parents usually blame each other. But it's not so simple.

A baby at birth is still attached to the mother by the umbilical cord. The cord is soon cut but the attachment remains. A child has little life of its own. To find and develop such a life is the greatest responsibility that we face. It's a life task but the teenage years are particularly crucial. Until now children can grow confident in the love lavished on them by their family. The teenage years, however, are a time when young people need to develop confidence in themselves. Ian's mother is shrewd enough to realise that whacks round the head, no matter how tempting, are not the best way of confirming him in self-worth.

No doubt our heavenly Father is tempted to give us a whack round the head (though at present he can see that we're doing that to each other) but, in the end, that will no more help us to grow than a whack round the head from his mother would help Ian.

To grow in self-confidence, self-worth, self-love is very difficult indeed. It's easy enough to appear self-confident – just put on the right clothes and wear the withering look that puts everyone down. But the appearances easily collapse and many teenagers, as well as adults, do eventually collapse under the strain of keeping up appearances.

A real sense of self-worth is a very different matter. Self-love, which is the opposite of self-centredness, is the beginning of adulthood and the beginning of following Jesus Christ. Jesus knew what he was saying when he repeated the greatest commandments as "to love the Lord your God with all your heart...and to love your neighbour as yourself." Love of self means appreciating ourselves for who we are – someone loved by God. This is the greatest gift we can receive and, ultimately, it is the gift of God.

Confirmation is a celebration of this gift. The celebration confirms the young person in the fact that he or she is personally loved by God and shares in the Spirit of God. It comes at a time when they are particularly in need of such reassurance. Confirmation prepares the young person for the adult world in which it is not enough to demand love but also give it. Such a perfect world in which everyone gives love and no-one demands it doesn't yet exist.

Your Child

THE COST OF LOVE

"Sometimes I wonder if I've done it wrong as a parent. Should I let him come and go as he wants and pretend I don't care? But I do care. He can't do just what he wants. When he gets married he's not going to be able to leave his plate on the table or clothes on the floor and expect someone to pick them up. We care because we love him — that's why we want him brought up properly."

Rosemarie — mother of a 19 year-old son

Your child is God's invitation – it is an invitation to become more like him – wanting to share love in a way that brings freedom to others.

AN INVITATION TO GROW A CLOSE

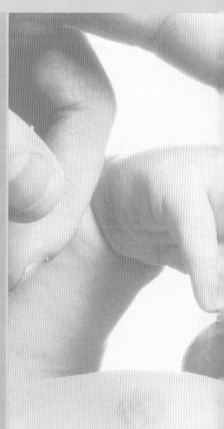

As children we wanted to be grown up and to do what grown-ups did – like going into pubs without being asked how old we were, smoking openly, driving expensive cars and enjoying sex. The trouble is that there is more to being "grown up" than those things. Adults often say that they didn't appreciate what their parents did for them until they themselves became parents. It's impossible for a child to imagine what it's really like being grown-up.

In the same way it's almost impossible for us to imagine what's it's like being God. We want to do the things we imagine he does – like controlling the world (which we think he does very badly) and having the freedom to do what he wants without people breathing down his neck giving him orders.

Being God is not like that. As we have seen, being God is very like being a parent. You appear to be in control but, if your children are to be free, you cannot possess them. You can't say to them: "Unless you do as I say I shall throw you out of the home and I don't want to ever see you again". You may be tempted, of course, to say this but, if you are to honour the dignity of your children, you can only continue to love them because that is the cost of love.

Most parents, like God, want the best for their children. Indeed, in what they want for their children, adults are often at their best.

LIKE PARENT, LIKE CHILD

Children grow to be like their parents. The similarities can, at the same time, be exasperating and endearing. It is well known that our own worst failings are those faults that we most dislike in others of the same sex; and this rule often applies between mother and daughter, and father and son. On the other hand, seeing oneself in the children can be wonderfully fulfilling...

"Victoria, the youngest, is spoilt. I feel sorry for her because she's really had no father and she's missed out with having to struggle to follow the others. She's like me – I was the youngest! I do the things my mother did, which I don't really like".

"Sometimes I find myself doing what my mother did; telling the children off in an Irish accent; or I spit on a hanky to clean their faces".

"My father has a strong influence on our children. Seeing my father with them makes me think about my own childhood and I appreciate him more as a person and feel closer to him. I also realise how I was responsible for some of the problems in my childhood – for example, I used to set my parents off against each other".

"I've discovered 'it's different when it's your own child'. I always thought this was a cliche but it's true."

"The biggest worry is that Jackie wants everything today. I find it very difficult to control my anger and any effort to discipline her doesn't seem to work. She comes back ten minutes later just as naughty. I admit, in many ways, she's like me".

O GOD

This is why it is the hope of Jesus that we will grow to be like our heavenly Father. Growing like God is as real a hope as a child growing to be like his or her parent. But this does take time. It would be as unreal for God to expect us to be like him as it would for parents to expect a young child to behave like an adult.

Jesus spoke of this hope frequently. He said that "if anyone serves me, my Father will honour him". He looked forward to the day when we share in God's glory:

"Father, I want those you have given me to be with me where I am, so that they may always see the glory you have given me before the foundation of the world."

The Perfect Child

"An argument started between the followers of Jesus about which of them was the greatest. Jesus knew what thoughts were going through their minds, and he took a little child and set him by his side and then said to them, 'Anyone who welcomes this little child in my name welcomes me; and anyone who welcomes me welcomes the one who sent me. For the least among you all, that is the one who is great'."

Jesus could only have known what thoughts were going through the minds of his followers because he himself had experienced such thoughts. It was very tempting for him to take the easy way out of this world and use the full force of strength at his disposal. At his trial Jesus said that "if my kingdom were of this world my men would have fought to prevent my being handed over to the Jews: but my kingdom is not of this kind."

The strength of Jesus Christ is his love. He lived a life of fulfilment without smoking, driving expensive cars, or casual sex (though his critics said Jesus drank too much). He was happy because he was totally free to give himself to others – like a little child.

Parents, like Jesus Christ, are often tempted not to bother. It's a life of giving, sometimes with little or nothing in return. But most parents would echo the words of Rosemarie who began this section: "There are times I wish I hadn't bothered with children – but if I had my life again I'd still do the same thing."

GROWING TOWARDS GOD

takes a lifetime. God loves us into maturity and looks forward to the day when he can talk to us almost as equals.

This is our heavenly Father's ambition for his children just as it is the ambition of every parent. Jesus came down to our level in order to raise us up to God's level.

The stages of our growth towards God are similar to the stages of our growth into human maturity. They are stages we all have to "go through" in order to grow up. Our growth in prayer – so that we can talk to God almost as an equal – begins from the moment of conception.

Before birth

Unity with God isn't something we have to arrange, choose or find; it already "is" a fact of our existence. Just as an unborn child in the silence of the womb is within the mother so we helpless dependent children are within God, within the all-embracing care and protection of his love. It is a world of silence filled only by God's love.

Infancy

After birth our "talking" consists of the odd gurgle, the loud scream and then, eventually, the first word: "Mummy" or "Daddy". Our vocabulary is limited and so is our understanding. We are loved by God just as parents love their baby; but as a baby we hardly know or appreciate what this means or how to respond to it. We may say the occasional word to God but there's a lot of screaming, too.

Childhood

As we grow older we children begin to chatter endlessly to God. Our minds are rushing here and there to try to tell God as quickly as we can about what we need. We're like the child coming home from school who can't wait to tell his or her mother all that's on the mind. All this chatter is important for the child but can be a little frustrating for the parent!

Adolescence

This is the stage at which so many of us remain stuck. It's the stage of trying to assert our independence of God. We may offer the occasional nod in his direction but, basically, we find the Parent a nuisance or irrelevant. God's love remains as he shows himself in the love we experience, in his creation and in the life of his Son, Jesus Christ. But we are impatient to be away and imagine we can go it alone.

Adulthood

Our failures at the adolescent stage can swamp us in in despair and weariness. And now it is, for the first time, that we are "still" enough to listen to God. We listen to God the way we listen to anyone else, by taking his words seriously. The words of Jesus are there waiting for us in the scriptures. When we read them or recall them, and take them seriously, we are listening to God. Yet this first adult discovery of God's love can disturb us. We begin to wonder if we are really worth it. We become afraid of making mistakes or fearful that if God really knew us he wouldn't like us.

GROWING T

Maturity

This is the final stage of our growth in prayer – our growth towards God – when we can return to the silence of the womb, surrounded by God's love yet now able to return his love with love which is true and trustful. This is a love in which we meet God face to face. We can look forward to such love in eternal life but we can glimpse it in this life. We need only to accept our weakness, accept the need for change in our lives and accept that God is constantly loving us into images of himself.